Enlightening
TIPS for the
"GO GETTERS"

FRED BROOKS JR.

Self Publish-n-30 DAYS
This Is The Year For Your New Book

www.selfpublishn30days.com

Published by *Self Publish -N- 30 Days*

Printed in the United States of America
ISBN: 978-1721782802
1. Entrepreneur 2. Self Help
Fred Brooks Jr. and F Brooks Enterprises.

Disclaimer/Warning:

This book is intended for lecture and entertainment purposes only. The author or publisher does not guarantee that anyone following these steps will be successful. The author and publisher shall have neither liability responsibility to anyone with respect to any loss or damage cause, or alleged to be caused, directly or indirectly by the information contained in this book.

In Loving Memory of my Sister
ALDREMA "NEICY" CARTER-VESSEL
Sunrise: June 9, 1967 – Sunset: July 21, 2011

"You left a lasting positive impact on the lives of many and you will never be forgotten."

—Fred Brooks Jr.

(Image source: lingomingo.com)

Go to:

http://www.nationalbreastcancer.org/breast-cancer-awareness-month

to support breast cancer awareness.

Contact me via email, phone, or web for consulting purposes:

AUTHOR: FRED BROOKS

Houston, TX

F|B

Phone: 713-364-8191

Email: fredbrooksjrtherealtor@gmail.com

Web: https://www.facebook.com/fredbrooksjrtherealtor/

IG: @fredbrooksjrtherealtor

INTRODUCTION

How do I achieve greatness and success?

If you are a "go getter," this is a question that you have asked yourself over and over again.

"Being a 'go getter' is a mindset."

It is not based on your background, your race or ethnicity, or your position in life. All "go getters" want to be great and successful, and they want to know what it takes to get there. Sometimes we as human beings over complicate processes that are truly simple to grasp.

I, personally, have been guilty of overcomplicating things in the past; especially when faced with situations that seemed impossible to overcome.

First, the most important tip is to have faith. Above all else, have faith. I have learned over the course of my life that I did not have to have all of the answers, or have every area of my life figured out. Honestly, I would have never imagined that I would be writing a book in 2018.

At an early age, I struggled with a lung condition. This condition eventually took away things that I loved including some sports activities. After visiting multiple physicians I had been told that most individuals with my condition did not survive to see age 26. At that time I was approximately age 15. I didn't have much faith back then, but my mother and father did. Their faith strengthened my faith.

As I write to you today I am currently age 36, and have not had any major complications from the condition that doctor's said I would not be able to overcome. I am 100% confident that I'm here today as a result of my faith.

Secondly, trusting yourself and gaining self confidence is almost as important as having faith. Sometimes the things that prevents us from taking on new tasks or stepping into new opportunities are fear and uncertainty. We have gotten so used to being comfortable in our situations, that we don't see that the situations we are so comfortable with, are handicapping us and preventing us from soaring to new heights.

Growing up in the Baton Rouge, LA area, my end game was to land a stable job at one of the petrochemical manufacturing plants. I had even gotten my Associate's Degree in Process Operations Technology. The job was comfortable, I knew what I would be doing every day, and I knew who I would be working with daily.

Don't get me wrong, working in the plant paid a lot of money and it was a respectable job, but given my prior lung condition, I was putting myself at risk for the sake of comfort. My problem back then was that I did not have the confidence and trust in myself to take on something completely new because of fear. After overcoming that fear and non-trust in myself I moved into Business Operations and Sales Operations where I have been growing over the last 12 years.

Next, networking is key.

"Change your circle, change your life."

Go getters only excel around other go getters. Please remember this as this simple statement can be a guide, and help you examine your circle. You have to be around people that will push you and vice versa. Stepping out of your comfort zone often takes a little shove from a like minded individual. We have all heard the phrase "iron sharpens iron." Hang around successful people long enough and you will most likely learn their exact methods of achieving their success. You have more control over life than you think you do, and it starts with controlling your circle.

Moving to Houston, TX, made it a little easier for me to examine and trim my circle, I am thankful for that. It also gave me the opportunity to meet new amazing people, and incur new amazing opportunities, which I am also thankful for. I have learned that in business and in life, you do not have to know how to complete each and every task yourself.

You just have to have ambition, and build strong relationships with good people that know how to complete those tasks. Additionally, your network should be trusting. You do not want to relinquish any amount of control in something that you hold dear, to someone whom is untrustworthy.

Finally, a go getter must be able to think strategically and intentionally. If you are not careful, your thoughts can wander.

> *"Wandering thoughts can often
> lead to negative thoughts."*

We are what we think we are. Thinking strategically and intentionally means gaining control of your thoughts, which will ultimately drive your actions. Material possessions are not a good indicator of how successful a person is; those things fade.

Also, if you are continuing to try to "keep up with the Joneses" you will never find happiness. God gave you another day to make an impact in someone else's life. If you took steps to go out and make that impact, and you were able to positively impact someone's life today, then you did what you set out to do. In my opinion, that's success.

In 2005 I got into a bad car accident which led to a major surgery on my left elbow. My thoughts at that time were as follows: I will never be able to use this arm again, I will have a hard time finding a job, my girlfriend is going to leave because I am a burden, I will never be able to get a place of my own, how will I drive, etc. Well, it's 13 years later and guess what......my arm is in good shape! I have had great job opportunities, my girlfriend is now my wife. We have been blessed with a great home in Houston!

I have been able to drive since 2006 and have held a commercial driver's license ever since, and I contribute it to controlling my thoughts and thinking strategically and intentionally.

If you or another go getter that you know has been struggling to find greatness, don't count yourself out. Better yet don't fear! I have results based tips for you that will help you answer the question on how to achieve greatness and success, eliminate the fear that comes with stepping out of your comfort zone, and guide you through the challenges you may face in daily walks of life.

TIP TOPIC 1:
HAVE FAITH

1.) IN ALL THINGS TRUST GOD:

Trust in the LORD with all your heart and lean not on your own understanding; in all your ways submit to him and he will make your paths straight.

—Proverbs 3:5-6

2.) LISTEN TO TESTIMONIES:

There is power in testimonies as it makes your faith stronger. Listening to testimonies of others increases and strengthens your confidence in God that what he is able to do for others, he can do for you.

(https://richardbejah.com/10-quick-tips-faith/)

3.) STAND STRONG AND BE PATIENT:

When you have faith, success is just a matter of time.
It can transform the poorest of the poor into
the richest of the rich.

(Thomas C. Corley; richhaits.net/what-is-faith-and-why-is-it-fundamental-to-success/)

4.) SPEAK IT INTO EXISTENCE:

Be clear about what you want. Faith wavers when it is uncertain what to claim. Claim what you want!

(Suzanne Evans; http://www.businessinsider.com/4-tips-to-building-a-successful-business-built-on-faith-2011-7)

5.) UNDERSTAND THAT FAITH IS THE KEY:

Entrepreneurship is not possible without faith. It's just not possible to be in control of a situation of uncontrollable elements, and still be confident in your ability to control it without a belief in a power outside of yourself.

(Aniruddha Atul Bhagwat; https://www.entrepreneur.com/article/292179)

6.) TAKE THE FIRST STEP AND BELIEVE:

Plant your seed in the ground, water it every day and believe. This is what allowed me to be in the position I am in right now. I would not stop believing.

(Tyler Perry; https://mic.com/articles/82459/11-very-successful-business-people-who-had-a-tough-time-in-their-20s#.Zt8zkyvqH)

7.) LISTEN TO FAITH BASED PODCASTS:

There is a wealth of uplifting podcast available that can help build your faith and put you in the right mindset.

For example: I found myself being in a negative mindset at work due to certain circumstances. I started listening to faith based podcasts at work

(Ralph Douglas West Ministries & Joel Osteen are both great ones.).

I learned how to focus on what God can do in my life, and not those circumstances. This allows me to have a stress free day at work.

(F. Brooks)

8.) DON'T FRET:

While observing the life of successful individuals, it can be easy to doubt yourself and feel like those individuals have something that you are lacking, or that you don't have the tools you need to succeed. Do not let that worry you. None of us are perfect and none of us has it all figured out.

You don't have to be perfect, but you do have to be willing. If you remain willing, hopeful, and trust God, then the right people, opportunities, and situations will align in your favor.

(F. Brooks)

9.) DON'T BE AFRAID TO MAKE MISTAKES:

In life we all make mistakes. The great thing is that our mistakes are our greatest teachers. Mistakes teach us to learn, do, and think differently. With that being said, it is human nature to make mistakes and those mistakes do not define us or our success. Our mistakes are already forgiven and we are blessed and successful because of God's grace, mercy, and favor.

(F. Brooks)

10.) DON'T BE AFRAID TO SEEK HELP:

Plans fail for lack of counsel, but with many advisers they succeed.

—Proverbs 15:22 NIV

11.) COUNT YOUR BLESSINGS:

*Remember what God has done for others and
what he has done for you in the past.
When people are facing difficult challenges, there is that
tendency to feel God is far away and doesn't care.
That's when you should sit down and count all
that he has done in the past.*

(https://richardbejah.com/10-quick-tips-faith/)

12.) FASTING IS A POWERFUL TOOL, USE IT:

Fasting makes you abandon yourself and your challenges to God. That focus on God alone is faith.

(https://richardbejah.com/10-quick-tips-faith/)

13.) DO NOT LET CIRCUMSTANCES STRESS YOU OUT, GOD IS IN CONTROL:

For I know the plans I have for you, declares the LORD, plans to prosper you and not harm you, plans to give you hope and a future.

—Jeremiah 29:11 NIV

14.) FIND JOY IN EVERY SITUATION:

Wherever you might be and whatever you might be up against, find joy. Have the maturity to seek joy in the ordinary and difficult, and believe that God hears you and will make room for you.

(Brittany Rust, Finding Joy In the Ordinary)

15.) DEPENDENCE ON YOURSELF ALONE IS INSUFFICIENT:

*Sure we're good at doing something, sure we're now professionals and number one in the category,
but you know what, our strongest point does not even reach God's weakest point.*

If you believe that what you're doing, you're doing it for the Glory of God, then He will lift you up and He will make you exceed your own capabilities and strength.

(https://livetopleasegod.wordpress.com/2013/04/21/ never-depend-on-your-own-strength-or-yourself/)

ENTREPRENEUR NOTE

_____

_____

_____

_____

_____

_____

_____

_____

_____

_____

_____

ENTREPRENEUR NOTE

_____

_____

_____

_____

_____

_____

_____

_____

_____

_____

ENTREPRENEUR NOTE

_____

_____

_____

_____

_____

_____

_____

_____

_____

_____

_____

ENTREPRENEUR NOTE

_____

_____

_____

_____

_____

_____

_____

_____

_____

_____

_____

BUILD SELF CONFIDENCE AND TRUST YOURSELF

1.) IF IT MAKES YOU HAPPY, IT CAN MAKE YOU SUCCESSFUL:

The first rule of success in any undertaking in life is to trust yourself. You won't get anywhere in life if you don't trust yourself. Do what it takes to make you happy. You are the only YOU that you have!

(http://www.warriorforum.com/mind-warriors/658764-trust-yourself-major-key-success.html)

Fred Brooks Jr.

2.) PRACTICE BEING BOLD AND COURAGEOUS:

Have the courage to follow your heart and intuition. They somehow know what you truly want to become.

(Steve Jobs; https://www.themuse.com/advice/25-steve-jobs-quotes-that-will-change-the-way-you-workin-the-best-way-possible)

3.) PUT ONE FOOT FORWARD:

Trusting in yourself is just as important as having faith. Individuals, especially highly successful individuals, do not want to waste their time coaching, mentoring, or helping people who do not put one foot forward toward helping themselves. Trusting yourself means having or finding the confidence to take the first step regardless of where it will lead.

(F. Brooks)

4.) COMMIT TO GOALS AND BELIEVE THAT YOU ARE A WINNER:

When winners set a goal, nothing gets in their way of achieving it. They commit 100 percent to the outcome, knowing that one difference between winners and losers is that winners commit to a goal and don't stop until they achieve it.

(https://moneypacers.com/2017/01/09/ successful-people-think/)

5.) STOP BEING YOUR OWN WORST CRITIC:

Eliminate negative self talk. None of us are perfect. Spend more time focusing on the positive and less time comparing yourself to others. If you start thinking success and speaking success into your life, you will become successful. Your words have power.

(F. Brooks)

6.) TURN NEGATIVITY INTO FUEL:

Let doubt and outside discouragement motivate you instead of depress you. There is no better confidence builder than being successful in an area where your peers, or strangers discounted your abilities.

(F. Brooks)

7.) ACT THE PART:

Your body language can instantly demonstrate self-assuredness, or it can scream insecurity. Present yourself in a way that says you are ready to master or take command of any situation.

(Jacqueline Whitmore; https://www.entrepreneur. com/article/247353#)

8.) DRESS THE PART:

When you look better, you feel better.
Look like the part you want to play, in other words, suit
up for success. Don't be afraid to let your personality
shine in your accessories.

(https://www.entrepreneur.com/article/247353#)

9.) TAKE ACTION:

Inaction breeds doubt and fear, while action breeds confidence and courage. Walk up to a stranger at a networking event, or accept a project you'd normally reject. Practice being self-confident and soon it will become second nature.

(https://www.entrepreneur.com/article/247353#)

10.) INCREASE COMPETENCE:

How do you feel more competent? By becoming more competent. And how do you do that? By studying and practicing. Just do small bits at a time. If you want to be a more competent writer, for example, don't try to tackle the entire profession of writing all at once. Just begin to write more.

(https://zenhabits.net/25-killer-actions-to-boost-your-self-confidence/)

11.) FACE YOUR FEAR:

A lack of self-confidence is simply a surplus of fear. You don't feel confident in your abilities because you fear the outcome.

To build self-confidence you need to pinpoint exactly what you fear. This way, when you realize what it is, you can begin the process of overcoming it.

(https://www.pickthebrain.com/blog/7-ultimate-ways-to-build-self-confidence/)

12.) DON'T FEAR FAILURE:

Failure is a natural part of life.

Not one man or woman ever set foot on this earth and left it without facing failure. So, give yourself a break and embrace failure, because only through failures will you find true success and true self-confidence.

(https://www.pickthebrain.com/blog/7-ultimate-ways-to-build-self-confidence/)

13.) FOLLOW YOUR HEART & INTUITION:

It takes a lot of courage to follow where the heart leads, especially when the ego/rational mind suggests you do not, but it also takes a lot of faith in oneself to do so. Therefore, listening to your intuition will strengthen the trust you have in yourself, allowing you to further rely on your own strengths and abilities.

(http://www.planetofsuccess.com/blog/2011/how-to-trust-in-yourself/)

14.) SET YOURSELF UP TO WIN:

Too many people are discouraged about their abilities because they set themselves goals that are too difficult to achieve. Start by setting small goals for yourself that you can easily win.

Once you have built a stream of successes that make you feel good about yourself, you can then move on to harder goals. Make sure that you also keep a list of all your achievements, both large and small, to remind yourself of the times that you have done well.

(https://www.entrepreneur.com/article/281874)

15.) PUSH THROUGH SELF-LIMITING BELIEFS:

As children we think we can conquer the world, but somewhere between childhood and adulthood, our enthusiasm and natural inclinations to dream big are squashed.

Parents and teachers start imposing their own beliefs— about what we can and can't do in life—upon us. If the instructors at the FBI Academy were not pushing us past our self-limiting beliefs, they weren't doing their job.

(https://www.success.com/blog/7-mental-hacks-to-be-more-confident-in-yourself)

ENTREPRENEUR NOTE

_____

_____

_____

_____

_____

_____

_____

_____

_____

_____

ENTREPRENEUR NOTE

ENTREPRENEUR NOTE

_____

_____

_____

_____

_____

_____

_____

_____

_____

_____

ENTREPRENEUR NOTE

_____

_____

_____

_____

_____

_____

_____

_____

_____

_____

_____

TIP TOPIC 3:

NETWORK

1.) REACH OUT TO OTHER GO GETTERS:

In order to prepare for success you have to reach out to individuals that have been where you are trying to go, and have done what you are trying to do. Those people can help motivate you, keep you focused, and help propel you to the next level.

(F. Brooks)

2.) BRING SOMETHING TO THE TABLE:

When it comes to networking with top people, the way to genuinely capture their interest is to share something that seems exotic to them.

(Dorie Clark; https://www.inc.com/jessica-stillman/ how-to-network-with-super-successful-people.html)

That exotic thing can be something as simple as displaying your "go getter" attitude, and demonstrating passion towards your beliefs.

(F. Brooks)

3.) SURROUND YOURSELF WITH LIKE-MINDED PEOPLE:

You typically become more like the five people you hang out with the most, so choose wisely. Like-minded people tend to move forward together, and somewhat become accountability partners.

(Holly Rust; http://www.huffingtonpost.com/holly-rust/7-rules-successful-people_b_7764252.html)

4.) SEEK LONG TERM PRODUCTIVE RELATIONSHIPS:

Relationships build partnerships. The more people you meet, the more partnerships you have. Always network whether that be in person or online through social media.

(Holly Rust; http://www.huffingtonpost.com/holly-rust/7-rules-successful-people_b_7764252.html)

5.) NURTURE FRIENDSHIPS:

Networking is not a numbers game. It doesn't matter how many business cards you pass out or whom you can instantly impress. Instead, successful networking is the process of fostering friendships and cultivating genuine connections with clients, colleagues and peers.

(Jacqueline Whitmore; https://www.entrepreneur. com/article/240278#)

6.) ATTITUDE IS EVERYTHING:

If people sense a negative and/or unlikable attitude at first contact, chances are that a second and more pertinent meeting will not happen. If you are not someone that people like to be around, you have to evaluate yourself and find out how to become that person.

(F. Brooks)

7.) DO NOT WASTE TIME:

Spend time with fewer individuals. The first five minutes of a conversation at a networking event usually involve introductions and polite small talk. Only after you spend some time with someone can you discover his or her true personality and interests.

(Jacqueline Whitmore; https://www.entrepreneur. com/article/240278#)

8.) COMMUNICATION, COMMUNICATION, COMMUNICATION:

Practice good communication. Know and respect the relationship expectations and boundaries you establish with your contacts. You have to develop mutual trust and rapport to deepen a relationship. Match your communication level to that of the other person.

(Cynthia K. Stevens; https://www.washingtonpost. com/business/capitalbusiness/career-coach-keys- to-networking-success/2011/10/26/gIQAvHS7WM_ story.html?utm_term=.fad201842582)

9.) CONTROL THE ENVIRONMENT:

Be yourself. Meet people in settings where you feel comfortable. If you thrive on meeting new people, get out there and work the room.

(Cynthia K. Stevens; https://www.washingtonpost. com/business/capitalbusiness/career-coach-keys-to-networking-success/2011/10/26/gIQAvHS7WM_ story.html?utm_term=.fad201842582)

10.) LEARN ABOUT YOUR CONNECTIONS:

To be interesting you must first be interested in the people you're connecting with. Talk to someone about themselves and they'll listen for hours.

(Maria Elena Duron; https://www.allbusiness.com/ networking-success-21537-1.html)

11.) MAKE YOUR MOVE:

When networking, be the first to shake hands. Be the meeter and the greeter, act like the host and be helpful to people as they are arriving.

(Maria Elena Duron; https://www.allbusiness.com/ networking-success-21537-1.html)

12.) NETWORK FROM THE INSIDE OUT:

Start with people you know, then expand to their acquaintances and finally strangers after the process becomes second nature.

(Taunee Besson; http://www.careercast.com/career-news/six-tips-successful-networking)

13.) STEP OUT OF YOUR COMFORT ZONE:

Not everyone has an outgoing personality. However, if you step out of your comfort zone and put yourself in that uncomfortable situation of being outgoing and social, your chances of success will greatly improve.

(F. Brooks)

14.) BE DIVERSE:

Create a diverse network of people with whom you can share ideas and gain information. Nothing is as effective as bouncing ideas back and forth with another professional whom you admire.

(Susan M. Heathfield; https://www.thebalance.com/ tips-for-successful-business-networking-1917776)

15.) FIND THE BAR AT NETWORKING EVENTS:

Whether or not you're drinking, it's always a great idea to position yourself at the edge of the bar. If you position yourself a few steps from the bar, you can easily strike up a conversation as people turn with drink in hand.

(https://www.forbes.com/sites/yec/2014/07/22/17-tips-to-survive-your-next-networking-event/#7e0d8d267cd4)

16.) TREAT PEOPLE LIKE FRIENDS:

Would you go to a friend, interrupt his/her conversation, hand over a business card, talk about yourself and then walk away? Of course not. Treat new networking relationships as you'd treat your friendships. Build rapport and trust that business will happen.

(https://www.forbes.com/sites/yec/2014/07/22/17-tips-to-survive-your-next-networking-event/#7e0d8d267cd4)

ENTREPRENEUR NOTE

_____

_____

_____

_____

_____

_____

_____

_____

_____

_____

ENTREPRENEUR NOTE

_____

_____

_____

_____

_____

_____

_____

_____

_____

_____

_____

ENTREPRENEUR NOTE

_____

_____

_____

_____

_____

_____

_____

_____

_____

_____

ENTREPRENEUR NOTE

_____

_____

_____

_____

_____

_____

_____

_____

_____

_____

_____

TIP TOPIC 4:

THINK STRATEGICALLY & INTENTIONALLY

1.) COMMIT YOURSELF TO BEING INTENTIONAL:

Being intentional is committing yourself to your plan and taking active steps to fulfill it.

(https://keepthinkingbig.com/3-simple-but-powerful-ways-to-become-intentional/; Tony Lynch)

2.) CONCENTRATE YOUR EFFORTS:

Prepare your work outside; get everything ready for yourself in the field, and after that build your house.

— Proverbs 24:27 ESV

3.) DO YOUR RESEARCH:

Put on your reporter's hat and look for alternative, diverse sources of information about your company, your competitors, and your industry.

(Lauren Perkins; https://www.inc.com/lauren-perkins/three-essential-steps-to-thinking-strategically.html)

4.) INFLUENCE RATHER THAN BE INFLUENCED:

This means being proactive rather than reactive.

(http://www.evancarmichael.com/library/glenn-ebersole/Ten-Top-Benefits-of-Strategic-Thinking-and-Planning-For-Business-and-Not-For-Profit-Organizations.html; J. Glenn Ebersole Jr.)

5.) ANALYZE GROUP INFLUENCES ON YOUR LIFE:

Closely analyze the behavior that is encouraged, and discouraged, in the groups to which you belong. For any given group, what are you "required" to believe? What are you "forbidden" to do? Every group enforces some level of conformity. Most people live too much within the view of themselves projected by others.

(http://www.criticalthinking.org/pages/critical-thinking-in-everyday-life-9-strategies/512)

6.) IDENTIFY ADDITIONAL OPPORTUNITIES:

By thinking more strategically, we identify more opportunities. This can help us to understand what's right for business, our team and us.

(https://www.managersdigest.co.uk/2017/01/31/ positive-benefits-strategic-thinking/)

7.) CONTROL YOUR THINKING:

By learning to control your thinking and eliminate the thoughts that no longer serve you, you open yourself up to all the unlimited possibilities you're here to experience.

(Dale East; https://www.amazon.com/Intentional-Thinking-Control-Thoughts-Produce-ebook/dp/ B01N79I3KH)

8.) EXPECT WHAT YOU PROJECT:

Project positively and your expectation is the support for your positive energy stream. You must set the stage for the outcome you expect by doing what's necessary to make it happen. Project (think) positively and expect only the best.

(http://manifestyourdream.blogspot.com/2010/03/ expect-what-you-project.html; Ken Keicher)

9.) EMBRACE TRADEOFFS:

A great strategic mind understands that in order to get something, you need to give up something else. You can't get fit and healthy without giving up on junk food. You can't launch your small business without giving up on your personal time.

(http://branduniq.com/2016/how-to-think-strategically/)

10.) UNDERSTAND YOUR ENVIRONMENT:

Recognize threats and evaluate threats to avoid or minimize exposure. Recognize advantages and evaluate advantages so they can be utilized to their fullest.

(https://www.slideshare.net/cmoeinc/7-ways-to-apply-strategic-thinking-to-your-work-and-life)

11.) DEAL WITH YOUR EGO:

Egocentric thinking is found in the disposition in human nature to think with an automatic subconscious bias in favor of oneself.

Once you identify egocentric thinking in operation, you can then work to replace it with more rational thought through systematic self-reflection, thinking along the lines of: What would a rational person feel in this or that situation? What would a rational person do? How does that compare with what I want to do?

(http://www.criticalthinking.org/pages/critical-thinking-in-everyday-life-9-strategies/512)

12.) REDEFINE THE WAY YOU SEE THINGS:

We live in a world, both personal and social, in which every situation is "defined," that is, given a meaning. How a situation is defined determines not only how we feel about it, but also how we act in it, and what implications it has for us.

However, virtually every situation can be defined in more than one way. Many of the negative definitions that we give to situations in our lives could in principle be transformed into positive ones. We can be happy when otherwise we would have been sad.

(http://www.criticalthinking.org/pages/critical-thinking-in-everyday-life-9-strategies/512).

13.) ALIGN YOUR ACTIONS
WITH YOUR INTENT:

*Once you have identified your intent, you must constantly be thinking about that intent.
With that being said, your actions must always seek to advance that intent.*

(F. Brooks)

14.) AVOID DAILY DISTRACTIONS:

One of the biggest challenges we face today is finding time to think. Technology made us more connected, but also more distracted. We are able to multitask, but for no meaningful purpose. Strategy requires focus for long periods.

(http://branduniq.com/2016/how-to-think-strategically/)

15.) ENGAGE IN GENUINE CONVERSATIONS WITH OTHERS:

Ask others to explain their thought processes. According to Forbes, part of this process is surrounding yourself with people who think differently than you do.

After much practice and exposure to different thoughts and ideas, you will be able to improve your strategic thinking and be a better asset to your company, family, or even yourself.

(http://interpersonalskillsonline.com/ strategic-thinking)

ENTREPRENEUR NOTE

_____

_____

_____

_____

_____

_____

_____

_____

_____

_____

ENTREPRENEUR NOTE

_____

_____

_____

_____

_____

_____

_____

_____

_____

_____

ENTREPRENEUR NOTE

ENTREPRENEUR NOTE

_____

_____

_____

_____

_____

_____

_____

_____

_____

_____

CONCLUSION

There is no better time than the present to start putting these tips into practice. No matter what you set out to accomplish in life, the tips in this book can help you get on the right track and stay on the right track, to achieve greatness and overcome any obstacles.

We currently live in a society where we can easily become distracted due to every day demands, as well as the desire to fit in and be accepted. You may feel as though being a "go getter" means that you drive a certain vehicle, live in a certain house, wear a certain brand of clothing, work in a certain career, etc. Additionally, media (social or otherwise) can make you feel as though you are not successful if you don't have those things. That is not the case, and even though it can be difficult, try not to let those outside factors cause you to de-value yourself because you are already well-equipped to accomplish your goals and dreams.

It doesn't matter if you are a stay at home mom, an athlete trying to make it to the next level, a student working on his or her first degree, or whatever it is that you are pursuing, you just need to believe that you are already successful and practice speaking your success into existence. The moment that you adopt the "go getter" mindset, increase your faith, start trusting yourself, are open to networking, and think strategically and intentionally, I am confident that you will start experiencing life from a whole new perspective; the "go getter" perspective.

I pray that this book continues to positively encourage you and help you achieve success in every area of your life.

Made in the USA
Lexington, KY
12 May 2019